LEVEL
3

NATIONAL GEOGRAPHIC CHANNEL
GREAT
MIGRATIONS
Elephants

Laura Marsh

**NATIONAL
GEOGRAPHIC**

Washington, D.C.

For Jackie, Billy, Jane, and Lilly —L.F.M

Library of Congress Cataloging-in-Publication Data
Marsh, Laura F.
Great migrations. Elephants / by Laura Marsh.
p. cm.
Includes index.
ISBN 978-1-4263-0743-0 (pbk. : alk. paper) -- ISBN 978-1-4263-0744-7 (library binding : alk. paper)
1. African elephant--Migration--Juvenile literature. I. Title.
QL737.P98M3697 2010
599.67'41568--dc22
2010017961

Dollar Tree ISBN: 978-1-4263-2397-3

Cover, Carlton Ward Jr; 1, Carlton Ward Jr/CarltonWard.com; 2, Jason Prince/Shutterstock; 4 (CTR), Paul Souders/Corbis; 7, Carlton Ward Jr; 8 (UP), Carlton Ward Jr; 8 (LO), Carlton Ward Jr; 9 (UP), Carlton Ward Jr; 9 (LO), Carlton Ward Jr; 10, Jim Kruger/iStockphoto; 10 (INSET), Jason Prince/Shutterstock; 11 (UP), Carlton Ward Jr; 11 (LO), Carlton Ward Jr; 12-13, Winfried Wisniewski/Corbis; 14-15, Carlton Ward Jr; 16-17, Carlton Ward Jr; 16 (INSET), Jason Prince/Shutterstock; 17, Gerry Ellis/Minden Pictures/National Geographic Creative; 18, Gunnar Pippel/Shutterstock; 19, Carlton Ward Jr; 19 (INSET), Jason Prince/Shutterstock; 21, Michael Nichols/National Geographic Creative; 22 (LO CTR), Norie Quintos/National Geographic Creative; 24, Martin Harvey/Gallo Images/Corbis

**National Geographic supports K–12 educators with ELA Common Core Resources.
Visit natgeoed.org/commoncore for more information.**

Printed in the United States of America
15/KG/1

Table of Contents

Tough Travel. 6

Full Circle 8

Elephant Emergency. 14

Helping Mali Elephants. 20

What You Can Do 23

What animal . . .

Can travel up to 90 miles a day?

Has tusks used to dig for water and find food?

Is the largest land animal on Earth?

An elephant!

Sahara desert

Asia

Mali

Africa

Elephants live in Africa and Asia. This book is about the elephants that live on the southern border of the Sahara desert in Mali, West Africa.

How Do We Measure Up?

An African elephant is so big, it makes a six-foot-tall man look small.

Tough Travel

Mali elephants migrate farther than any other elephants. Scientists estimate they travel between 280 and 435 miles. Traveling 435 miles is like walking from Washington, D.C., to New York City and back every year!

Weird but true! Elephants sleep standing up.

435 miles round trip

Washington, D.C.

New York City

Elephant Mileage

Scientists are able to find out how far an elephant travels by attaching a GPS tracking collar around its neck. The elephant is given medicine to make it fall asleep so that the scientists can safely attach the collar. When the elephant wakes up, it joins the herd and goes on its way.

Full Circle

The Mali elephants start and end their journey at Lake Banzena. It contains the only year-round watering hole in the area. All other watering holes disappear during the dry season.

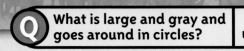

The elephants spend the dry season at Lake Banzena. But by April and May there is little food at Banzena because elephants and other animals have eaten it. It is time to move on.

When the rainy season begins, the elephants travel south. The rain renews old watering holes and allows nutritious new food to grow elsewhere.

Weighty Word

INSTINCT: Behavior that animals are born knowing how to do

Perfect Timing

The elephants begin their migration south as soon as the first rain begins. They know by instinct that it's time to migrate.

The elephants eat the plants around a small watering hole and then move on. They travel from watering hole to watering hole for many months. Their route makes a big circle.

By November, the rains stop and it's time to return to Lake Banzena, where they spend another dry season. But the elephants must hurry before the watering holes along the way dry up. They can't live without water.

weird but true! Elephants can drink up to 60 gallons of water a day.

Elephant Emergency

More than 1,000 elephants once roamed all across Mali. Now there are fewer than 400 elephants.

What happened to the Mali elephants?

Weird but true!

An elephant's tusks keep growing throughout its adult life.

1,000 elephants

400 elephants

Now

Then

= 100 elephants

15

Poachers killed many elephants in the 1970s and 1980s. They only wanted the elephants' tusks and sold them at high prices.

Although poaching is outlawed, it is still a problem today.

Weighty Word

POACHER: Someone who hunts animals illegally

An elephant's trunk has about 100,000 different muscles, but no bones.

Elephant tusks are made of ivory, which has been used to make things like jewelry and piano keys.

Mali elephants are trying to survive in difficult conditions. There is less water and fewer plants than there used to be. One reason is because the Earth has become warmer. Higher temperatures are drying up water sources.

But people are making it harder for elephants, too. They are settling where elephants live and migrate. So there is less and less land for the elephants. Also, livestock owned by local people are eating plants and drinking water that elephants need, too.

Q Why was the elephant asked to leave the swimming pool?

A He couldn't hold up his trunks.

Weighty Word

LIVESTOCK: Animals raised to sell or use

19

Helping Mali Elephants

Scientists are keeping track of the number of elephants so that if elephant numbers go down, they can find a solution before it's too late.

Scientists are also tagging elephants with special collars to track them. The collars show scientists exactly where the elephants travel. Then people can build roads and homes elsewhere. This will create safe migration paths for the elephants.

An elephant's skin can be one inch thick in some areas.

Local people in the Mali government want the elephants to survive. Mali children learn about the elephants in school. The more people know, the better we can help the elephants.

What You Can Do

To learn more about Mali elephants and their amazing migration, check out these organizations that help them.

National Geographic Society

kids.nationalgeographic.com/Animals/
CreatureFeature/African-elephant

Save the Elephants

savetheelephants.org

The WILD Foundation

www.wild.org/where-we-work/
the-desert-elephants-of-mali